CW00485635

# Did They Laugh?

– KENNETH PAYNE –

*A look at some of the amusing
passages in the Gospels*

Printed and bound in England by www.printondemand-worldwide.com

http://www.fast-print.net/bookshop

# DID THEY LAUGH?
Copyright © Kenneth Payne 2016

A catalogue record for this book is available from the British Library

ISBN 978-178456-408-7

First published 2016 by
FASTPRINT PUBLISHING
Peterborough, England.

# *Contents*

# Mooi postkantoor

**H**et behouden van een historisch pand is volgens projectontwikkelaars vaak te duur (Hotel Luijk); het slopen van een lelijk pand ook (KPN-gebouw Molenstraat). En zo verdwijnt in Oss het mooie en blijft de lelijkheid overeind.

Wie vanaf het spoor de Molenstraat in komt, kan het best naar links blijven kijken. Daar staan de fabrikantenvilla's uit het einde van de negentiende eeuw die stad en straat al heel lang aanzien. In het begin van de twintigste eeuw kon je ook heel goed naar rechts kijken. Daar stond vanaf het spoor de margarinefabriek van Meyer van Leeuwen met mooie neoklassieke ge-

## Stille Getuigen

**In de rubriek Stille Getuigen koppelt historicus John van Zuijlen actuele zaken uit de regio aan nieuws uit vroeger tijden.**

vels (1878) en daarnaast de koekfabriek van Ploegmakers (1917), met een iets pompeuzer maar toch karakteristiek aanzien. Daarna een rijtje keurige herenhuizen en dan het fraaie postkantoor uit 1904, villa Josina uit 1870, waar Jan Jurgens woonde, menten het project waaronder de plannen met het kasteel vallen. Die plannen omvatten onder andere de aanleg van een natuurgebied in de uiterwaard bij het kasteel, maar ook de aanleg van een geul vanaf de Maas naar het oude verdedigingswerk. „Op oude kaarten is te zien dat er een haven lag bij het kasteel. Dat was vooral om het kasteel te bevoorraden. Het is onze wens om dat in de toekomst terug te krijgen." Van Mierlo zegt het voorzichtig. De wens staat echter al wel op een kaart die onlangs werd verspreid. De kaart toont de ambities van waterschap, gemeente, Natuurmonumenten en Rijkswaterstaat voor het Maastraject Ravenstein- Lith. Op de kaart staan verschillende geulen die de oude meanders in de rivier nabootsen. Met de geulen is meer waterberging mogelijk en slinkt de kans op overstromingen. Een kleine haven voor waterrecreanten zou een mooie impuls geven aan het gebied rond Kas-

teel. Van Mierlo spreekt van een battenbos dat het blik aan het oo gaat onttrekken. Het oostelijk ne huis wordt in de plannen ook gr accommodatie, waardoor er stra totaal 32 mensen kunnen verblij

## Elk weekend vol

De uitbreiding van capaciteit is gewenst. Sinds Wilbert en Elle Schijndel vorig jaar begonnen m de exploitatie van het kasteel zij zes kamers bijna elk weekeinde zet geweest. „We zitten nu al to gend jaar november vol", meldt „En elke vrijdag van april tot ok is er hier een trouwceremonie", Wilbert aan.

„Het gaat gewoon hartstikke goed", vat Jan van Mierlo samer Niet vreemd vindt Elle. „Dit is v veel mensen nog een onbekend bied. Maar als ze eenmaal zijn g weest, zijn ze om. Een groep Du sers is hier zelfs al vier keer gew Ze vinden de omgeving zó moo

# *Acknowledgements*

There have been several books that have helped in completing this short incursion into the subject, and in particular:

"Humour and Irony in the New Testament" by Jacob Jonnson (Reykjavik, 1965)

"The Humour of Christ" by Elton Trueblood (Harper and Row, 1975)

"Between Heaven and Mirth" by James Martin, S.J. (Harper One, 2012)

"God and the World" by Pope Benedict (San Francisco, Ignatius Press)

A number of other people have contributed ideas, and I am extremely grateful to Alice Salczynska for designing the cover and Abina Bastin for typing and editing.

The readings are all taken from the New Revised Standard Version of the Bible used with permission.

# Chapter 1. Introduction:

M any years ago I was inspired by the preaching of Archbishop Roberts who was Archbishop of Bombay at the time. He was visiting various parishes in England and surprisingly I heard him in two different places preach exactly the same sermon, the subject of which was the disciples after the resurrection of Jesus, journeying towards Emmaus. Archbishop Roberts claimed that Jesus must have really been pulling their legs whilst walking along with them, not being recognised, and asking them questions about himself.

At the back of my mind I thought for many years about this and then came across a book published in Reykjavik by Jacob Jonnson, entitled "Humour and Irony in the New Testament". It was a massive and erudite volume in which I delved into a number of times over the years.

A third incident occurred when I was privileged to go to Jamaica and, also the Philippines, for short visits to help the Missionaries of the Poor in their caring for the homeless and destitute. I won't describe here the appalling condition of some of the people and the challenge to help, but one of the things that impressed me most was that the Brothers, and many of them were quite young, were doing horrific tasks in cleaning up and looking after the destitute and homeless. Then when we gathered together at supper in the evening we would talk and laugh and there would be, in contrast to the day's work, a great deal of fun and jokes banded around the table.

All this combined to convince me that when Jesus and the Apostles, who spent so much time engaged in healing sick people, when they got together to eat and share, as they must have done on many occasions, there would have been a great deal of laughter and fun. It was a very human reaction to the difficult tasks they were performing during the daytime. Unfortunately we hardly get a glimpse of that in the Gospel which is read with a serious face week after week. So I decided that it would be a worthwhile task to research some of the things that Jesus said and did.

There is of course one difficulty in attempting this, and that is appreciating the different culture and mindset of the people involved. Humour, after all, is linked closely with situations and topical events, so that what made people laugh 2,000 years ago in Palestine may not appear to us to be at all funny. However, with a little imagination we can probe into the thinking and reactions of both Jesus and his followers. Laughter depends upon culture and also on the period of history, and people laugh for different reasons. We need to be aware of the background and the tradition of the people concerned. Most of Jesus' teaching was to be expected and anticipated as the teaching of a Rabbi, and to make his point he would frequently lapse into irony and humour.

Even Pope Benedict who is a great scripture scholar, in "God and the World", has written:

"I believe (God) has a great sense of humour. Sometimes he gives you something like a nudge and says "don't take yourself so seriously". Humour is in fact an essential element in the mirth of creation. We can see how, in many matters in our lives, God wants to prod us into taking things a bit more lightly; to see the funny side of it, to get down off our pedestal and not to forget our sense of fun."

We are often so familiar with certain texts in the Gospels that we fail to see the humour, but Jesus expected others to laugh at some of the things he said. However, he is not telling a joke just in order to make people laugh but rather to impress upon them an important religious truth. I hope to illustrate this in subsequent chapters. Much of Christ's humour depends on a blend of ideas, and comical events that happen or that could happen, and these would appear to be funny in any language. Christ's humour is the humour of comedy, of surprise and of the absurd.

The Jewish Rabbi's way of teaching was frequently by exaggerating the point he wished to make, and often this would cause a smile from his hearers. It was also quite common to combine criticism with humour. Joy, humour and laughter are essential facets of the spiritual life of a Christian and stem immediately from the Gospel itself and from the life and teaching of Jesus. What follows is a random selection of examples of humour in the Gospels.

However, we should bear in mind G.K. Chesterton's view in the last line of his book, "Orthodoxy":

"There was some one thing that was too great for God to show us when he walked upon our earth; and I have sometimes fancied that it was His mirth."

# *Chapter 2 – Events*

## *The story of Zacchaeus – Lk 19,1-10*

*"He entered Jericho and was passing through it. A man was there named Zacchaeus; he was a chief tax collector and was rich. He was trying to see who Jesus was, but on account of the crowd he could not because he was short in stature. So he ran ahead and climbed a sycamore tree to see him, because he was going to pass that way. When Jesus came to the place he looked up and said by him, "Zacchaeus, hurry and come down; for I must stay at your house today". So he hurried down and was happy to welcome him. All who saw began to grumble and said, "He has gone to be the guest of one who is a sinner". Zacchaeus stood there and said to the Lord, "Look, half of my possessions, Lord, I will give to the poor; and if I have defrauded anyone of anything, I will pay them back four times as much". Jesus said to him, "Today salvation has come to this house because he too is a son of Abraham. For the Son of Man came to seek out and to save the lost". "*

Zacchaeus was a leading Tax Collector, a rich man probably hated by many. He was short but did not mind looking ridiculous by climbing up a tree in order to see Jesus, and this would have been quite comical as people in the crowd would have looked up to see him probably as he was revealing, beneath his loose fitting cloak, all that could be revealed.

## The Wedding at Cana – Jn 2, 1-5

*"On the third day there was a wedding in Cana of Galilee, and the mother of Jesus was there. Jesus and his disciples had also been invited to the wedding. When the wine gave out the mother of Jesus said to him, "They have no wine". And Jesus said to her, "Woman, what concern is that to you and to me? My hour has not yet come.""*

Jesus' words to his mother, based on a similar expression in the Old Testament, could mean, "What do you want me to do about it?" or "Why are you saying this?" Mary does not give up, but smiles, knowingly at the servants, telling them to do what her son says. The result is such a great quantity of wine that there must have been many resultant bursts of fun and laughter.

## The Samaritan Woman – Jn 4,7-18

*"It was about noon. A Samaritan woman came to draw water and Jesus said to her "Give me a drink." (His disciples had gone to the city to buy food.) The Samaritan woman said to him "How is it that you, a Jew, asks a drink of me, a woman of Samaria?" (Jews do not share things in common with Samaritans.) Jesus answered her, "If you knew the gift of God, and who it is that is saying to you, 'Give me a drink' you would have asked him, and he would have given you living water". The woman said to him, "Sir, you have no bucket, and the well is deep. Where do you get that living water? Are you greater than our ancestor Jacob, who gave us the well, and with his sons and his flock drank from it?" Jesus said to her, "Everyone who drinks of this water will be thirsty again, but those who drink of the water that I will give them will never be*

*thirsty. The water that I will give will become in them a spring of water gushing up to eternal life." The woman said to him, "Sir, give me this water, so that I may never be thirsty or have to keep coming here to draw water".*

*Jesus said to her, "Go call your husband and come back." The woman answered him, "I have no husband." Jesus said to her, "You are right in saying, 'I have no husband'; for you have had five husbands, and the one you have now is not your husband. What you have said is true!" The woman said to him, "Sir, I see that you are a prophet."*

John in his gospel is not much given to highlighting the amusing things that Jesus did or said. However, in the account of the meeting with the Samaritan woman at the well he must have raised a few eyebrows and the Apostles who were involved must have realised the revolutionary and somewhat amusing nature of the encounter at the well. There is irony in Jesus' dialogue with the women.

Whenever I think of this event in Jesus' life I recall Fr Richard Ho Lung's musical "The Rock" which was performed in Kingston, Jamaica several years ago, and for one of the performances some of the residents of the centres the brothers cared for were taken to see it. One scene we encountered the Samaritan woman at the well and part of the props for this was a big earthenware container used for carrying the water. Whilst the singers were singing an appropriate song "Give us living water", the earthenware pot was placed near the side of the stage. At this point one of the residents, Jack, suffering from Down's Syndrome, was sitting in the front row and suddenly leapt up onto the stage and started urinating into the pot. The electrician controlling the lights was unable to see what was happening, but decided that he should highlight whatever it was so he proceeded to direct a full beam of light on Jack who loved being in the limelight. Fr Ho Lung was back stage at the time and realised that something unusual was going on. He sent a helper to see and they immediately grabbed the earthenware pot and marched off the stage explaining, "There is liquid in it and it's warm". This is undoubtedly one of the things that Jesus would have laughed at today, in addition to his ironic comment to the women in the Gospel.

## *Doctors – Mk 5, 26*

*"She has endured much under many physicians, and had spent all that she had; and she was no better, but rather grew worse."*

Was the evangelist amazingly having a dig at the doctors or claiming that it had been impossible to cure her by ordinary means?

## *Martha and Mary – Lk 10,38-42*

*"Now as they went on their way, he entered a certain village, where a woman named Martha welcomed him into her home. She had a sister named Mary, who sat at the Lord's feet and listened to what he was saying. But Martha was distracted by her many tasks; so she came to him and asked, "Lord, do you not care that my sister has left me to do all the work by myself? Tell her then to help me." But the Lord answered her, "Martha, Martha, you are worried and distracted by many*

*things; there is need of only one thing. Mary has chosen the better part, which will not be taken away from her."*

Hospitality was usually shown in two ways: the sharing of food and the practice of listening to the Torah during the meal. Humour comes into this situation because Jesus addresses Martha in a double way: "Martha, Martha". The use of such a double address meant kindness and particularly playfulness, so one can be sure that Jesus was smiling and in a sense pulling Martha's leg.

## *Jesus Walks on Water – Matt 14, 25-26*

*"And early in the morning he came walking toward them on the sea. But when the disciples saw him, walking on the sea, they were terrified, saying, "It is a ghost!" And they cried out in fear."*

Peter is at first afraid, but then reacts with faith, but undoubtedly caused a laugh from the others when he began to sink and had to be hauled up over the side of the boat.

# *Chapter 3 – Parables*

## *A Great Banquet – Lk 13,29-30*

*"Then people will come from east and west, from north and south, and will eat in the kingdom of God. Indeed, some are last who will be first, and some are first who will be last".*

Jews believe that one day they would join Abraham, Isaac and Jacob and all the great prophets at a wonderful banquet. But here Luke gives a comical picture of the patriarchs having dinner with a whole lot of unwashed Gentiles from all over the world. The Gentiles were not to be the excluded ones but they would have their situation reversed: *"He who is last will be first and the first last".*

## *The Good Samaritan – Lk 10, 25-37*

*"Just then a lawyer stood up to test Jesus. "Teacher", he said, "what must I do to inherit eternal life?" He said to him, "What is written in the law? What do you read there?" He answered, "You shall love the Lord your God with all your heart and with all your soul, and with all your mind; and your neighbour as yourself." And he said to him, "You have given the right answer, do this, and you will live." But wanting to justify himself, he asked Jesus, "And who is my neighbour?" Jesus replied, "A man was going down from Jerusalem to Jericho, and fell into the hands of robbers, who stripped him, beat him, and went away leaving him half dead. Now by chance a priest was going down that road; and when he saw*

*him, he passed by on the other side. So likewise a Levite, when he came to the place and saw him, passed by on the other side. But a Samaritan while travelling came near him; and when he saw him he was moved with pity. He went to him and bandaged his wounds having poured oil and wine on them. Then he put him on his own animal, brought him to an inn, and took care of him. The next day he took out two denarii, gave them to the innkeeper, and said, 'Take care of him,; and when I come back, I will repay you whatever more you spend.' Which of these three, do you think, was a neighbour to the man who fell into the hands of the robbers?" He said, "The one who showed him mercy." Jesus said to him, "Go and do likewise.""*

The lawyer wanted to pose a problem to Jesus, who, nevertheless turned it round on him. Did the priest and the Levite not stop because they were both of a high social standing, like the lawyer himself? If this was the reason, it would have brought a smile on the face of the hearers. And that it was a Samaritan who showed compassion would have caused a gasp of amazement on the part of the lawyer,

## *The Power of the Small – Lk 13,19/13, 20-21/17,5-6*

*""It is like a mustard seed that someone took and sowed in the garden; it grew and became a tree, and the birds of the air made nests in its branches".*

*"And again he said, "To what should I compare the kingdom of God? It is like yeast that a woman took and mixed in with three measures of floor until all of it was leavened"."*

*"The Apostles said to the Lord "Increase our faith!" The Lord replied "If you had faith the size of a mustard seed, you*

*could say to this mulberry tree, 'Be uprooted and planted in the sea', and it would obey you."*

These are not exactly comical but they are surprising and would have generated a smile from the hearers. They underline an enormous hidden power which is not visible on the surface. Perhaps Jesus was hinting at the tremendous human energy expended by religious leaders thinking that the coming of the Kingdom would be by their own efforts, and this is not so. In modern terms it is more like the hidden power in an atom, which, given the right circumstances, can explode and release great power.

## *The Widow and the unjust Judge – Lk 18,1-8*

*Then Jesus told them a parable about their need to pray always and not to lose heart. He said, "In a certain city there was a judge who neither feared God nor had respect for people. In that city there was a widow who kept coming to him and saying, 'Grant me justice against my opponent.' For a while he refused; but later he said to himself, 'Though I have no fear of God and no respect for anyone, yet because this widow keeps bothering me, I will grant her justice, so that she may not wear me out by continually coming.' " And the Lord said, "Listen to what the unjust judge says. And will not God grant justice to his chosen ones who cry to him day and night? Will he delay long in helping them? I tell you, he will quickly grant justice to them. And yet, when the Son of Man comes, will he find faith on earth?"*

This recounts a story of a woman repeatedly running to the door of an official until at last she wins the battle with her request. This must have caused laughter amongst the lower classes of people who listened to Jesus and possibly also the colleagues of the judge.

## *The Ten Virgins – Matt 25,1-12*

*"Then the kingdom of heaven will be like this. Ten bridesmaids took their lamps and went to meet the bridegroom. Five of them were foolish, and five were wise. When the foolish took their lamps they took no oil with them; but the wise took flasks of oil with their lamps. As the bridegroom was delayed, all of them became drowsy and slept. But at midnight there was a shout, 'Look! Here is the bridegroom! Come out to meet him.' Then all those bridesmaids got up and trimmed their lamps. The foolish said to the wise, 'Give us some of your oil, for our lamps are going out'. But the wise replied, 'No! there will not be enough for you and for us; you had better go to the dealers and buy some for yourselves.' And while they went to buy it, the bridegroom came, and those who were ready went with him into the wedding banquet; and the door was shut. Later the other bridesmaids came also, saying, 'Lord, lord, open to us'. But he replied, 'Truly I tell you, I do not know you.' Keep awake therefore, for you know nether the day nor the hour."*

In modern terms it may be the case that the man having arrived too late for the ceremony, it has to begin without him. He has been left outside and this could be seen as comical.

## *The unfortunate friend – Lk 11,5-8*

*"And he said to them, "Suppose one of you had a friend, and you go to him at midnight and say to him, 'Friend, lend me three loaves of bread, for a friend of mine has arrived and I have nothing to set before him.' And he answers from within,*

*'Do not bother me; the door has already been locked, and my children are with me in bed; I cannot get up and give you anything.' I tell you even though he will not get up and give him anything because he is his friend, at least because of his persistence he will get up and give him whatever he needs."*

It was not unusual for visitors to call in during the night when people were used to being disturbed. However, in the example Jesus gives, where the friend is asking for bread, it would mean waking up his wife and probably his family as well, and then for his wife to bake some more bread because bread was never kept over from the previous day, it was always fresh. Jesus gives it as an example of perseverance in prayer, but in fact it is a comical situation.

## The Marriage Feast – Matt 22,1-14

*Once more Jesus spoke to them in parables, saying: "The kingdom of heaven may be compared to a king who gave a wedding banquet for his son. He sent his slaves to call those who had been invited to the wedding banquet, but they would not come. Again he sent other slaves, saying 'Tell those who have been invited: Look I have prepared my dinner, my oxen and my fat calves have been slaughtered, and everything is ready; come to the wedding banquet.' But they made light of it and went away, one to his farm, another to his business, while the rest seized his slaves, mistreated them and killed them. The king was enraged. He sent his troops, destroyed those murderers, and burned their city. Then he said to his slaves, 'The wedding is ready, but those invited were not worthy. Go out therefore into the main streets, and invite everyone you find to the wedding banquet." Those slaves went out into the streets and gathered all whom they found, both good and bad; so the wedding hall was filled with guests.*

*"But when the king came in to see the guests, he noticed a man there who was not wearing a wedding robe and he said to him, 'Friend, how did you get in here without a wedding robe?' And he was speechless. Then the king said to the attendants, 'Bind him hand and foot, and throw him into the outer darkness, where there will be weeping and gnashing of teeth.' For many are called, but few are chosen.'"*

"By wedding garments" is probably meant "clean clothes", and it meant that someone had turned up in overalls or in their dirty working clothes. Such would have been a serious offence as well as being amusing for the spectators.

## The call of Nathanael – Jn 1,43-50

*The next day Jesus decided to go to Galilee. He found Philip and said to him, "Follow me". Now Philip was from Bethsaida, the city of Andrew and Peter, Philip found Nathanael and said to him, "We have found him about whom Moses in the law and also the prophets wrote, Jesus son of Joseph from Nazareth." Nathanael said to him, "Can anything good come out of Nazareth?" Philip said to him, "Come and see". When Jesus saw Nathanael coming toward him, he said of him, "Here is truly an Israelite in whom there is no deceit!" Nathanael asked him, "Where did you get to know me?" Jesus answered, "I saw you under the fig tree before Philip called you." Nathanael replied, "Rabbi, you are the Son of God! You are the King of Israel!"*

One can easily miss the humour with this encounter between Jesus and Nathanael. Nathanael's remark: "Can anything good ever come from Nazareth?" This is rather like asking if anything good can come from Isis or one of the towns occupied by them in Syria. Galileans were not a very highly esteemed people and their religious practice was somewhat tainted, as their dialect made it somewhat difficult to recite prayers in good Hebrew. Later Nathanael was quite amazed at Jesus' peculiar gifts, for example when he said he saw him under the fig tree, when Jesus joyfully reminds him that this is nothing compared to greater things that he would see later.

## The treasure in the field – Matt 13, 44

*"The kingdom of heaven is like a treasure hidden in a field, which someone found and hid; then in his joy he goes and sells all that he has and buys the field."*

The humour here is in the cleverness of the man who kept secret his knowledge of the whereabouts of the treasure.

## The old ways and the new – Lk 5, 33-39

*"Then they said to him, "John's disciples, like the disciples of the Pharisees, frequently fast and pray, but your disciplines eat and drink. Jesus said to them, "You cannot make wedding guests fast while the bridegroom is with them, can you? The days will come when the bridegroom will be taken away from them and then they will fast in those days." He also told them a parable; "No one tears a piece from a new garment and sews it on to an old garment; otherwise the new will be torn, and the piece from the new will not match the old. And no one puts new wine into old wineskins; otherwise the new wine will burst the skins and will be spilled, and the skins will be*

*destroyed. But new wine must be put into fresh wineskins. And no one after drinking old wine desires new wine, but says, 'The old is good.' "*

In a semi humorous way Jesus makes the point that there is to be a revolution in thought. He is attacking those who say "We have always done it that way".

Elton Trueblood in his book "The Humour of Christ" makes the point that we should be grateful to Luke for keeping this final touch to the story of the wineskins, which are incomplete in Matthew and Mark's Gospels. Luke gives the real punch line of the story but it often goes unnoticed and readers think that Christ is arguing that the old ways are intrinsically better. No, with a smile, he is saying that there must be a new start.

## *The Prodigal Son – Lk 15,11-12*

*Then Jesus said, "There was a man who had two sons. The Younger of them said to his father, 'Father, give me the share of the property that will belong to me.' So he divided his property between them.*

There would seem to be a certain comic turn to this parable, it being quite ridiculous that a person only remembers his father and his old home when he was in trouble This would have caused quite a smile on Jesus' hearers.

## *The Rich Fool – Lk 12,13-21*

*"Someone in the crowd said to him, "Teacher, tell my brother to divide the family inheritance with me." But he said to him, "Friend, who set me to be a judge or arbitrator over*

you?" And he said to them, "Take care! Be on your guard against all kinds of greed; for one's life does not consist in the abundance of possessions." Then he told them a parable: "The land of a rich man produced abundantly. And he thought to himself, 'What should I do for I have no place to store my crops?' Then he said, 'I will do this: I will pull down my barns and build larger ones, and then I will store all my grain and my goods. And I will say to my soul, 'Soul, you have ample goods laid up for many years; relax, eat, drink be merry. But God said to him, ' You fool! This very night your life is being demanded of you. And the things you have prepared, whose will they be?' So is with those who store up treasures for themselves but are not rich towards God."*

The Hebrews knew what money was worth: "Three things injure the body: heartache, stomach trouble and an empty purse, which is the worst?" Based on this there are many stories about a man planning for the future with the angel of death intervening. There is a father of a child who had just been circumcised saying that he is setting aside some wine for the boy's wedding days. He had in fact only thirty days to live. Another story of a shoemaker who made a pair of shoes that would last him seven years. The angel of death laughed because he knew the man had only seven days to live. Jesus was undoubtedly well aware of these stories.

# *Chapter 4 – Teachings*

M any of the guidelines that Jesus gave his followers are based on very well known sayings. For the most part they have become common parlance to us and we fail to note the humour embedded in them.

## *Hiding Light – Matt 5,15*

*"No one after lighting a lamp puts it under the bushel basket, but on the lamp-stand, and it gives light to all in the house."*

In modern parlance we are not to put our bedside lamp underneath the bed as this would appear comical and useless.

## *Swearing – Matt 5, 36*

*"And do not swear by your head, for you cannot make one hair white or black."*

Man is unable to change God's creation. It would be like trying to live at the bottom of the sea without any supply of oxygen. This would be impossible.

## *Figs from Thistles – Matt 7,16/Lk 6,44*

*"You will know them by their fruits. Are grapes gathered from thorns, or figs from thistles?"*

*"For each tree is known by its own fruit. Figs are not gathered from thorns nor are grapes picked from a bramble bush."*

Instead one could say that one does not gather potatoes from dandelions. This would appear today to be more comical.

## Prayer – Matt 6,7

*"When you are praying, do not heap up empty phrases as the Gentiles do; for they think that they will be heard because of their many words."*

A long prayer was considered more effective than a short one, and especially if it was heard by lots of people. Jesus ridicules this idea.

## Speck and Log in the Eye – Matt 7,3/Lk 6,41

*"How can you say to your neighbour, let me take the speck out of your eye, while the log is in your own eye?"*

*"Why do you see the speck in your neighbour's eye, but do not notice the log in your own eye?"*

This reminds me of the lady who complained about the appalling state of her neighbour's kitchen when in fact it was her own windows that were dirty.

## The Camel through the Eye of a Needle – Matt 19,24/Mk 10, 25/Lk 18,25

*"Again I tell you, it is easier for a camel to go through the eye of a needle than for someone who is rich to enter the kingdom of God,"*

Some commentators suggest that it was a case of passing a cable through the eye of a needle. If Jesus had been speaking today he might have said that it was more difficult to transport the Eiffel Tower through the Channel Tunnel than it would be for a rich man to enter the Kingdom of Heaven.

## *The widow's offering – Mk 12, 41-44*

*"He sat down opposite the treasury, and watched the crowd putting money into the treasury. Many rich people put in large sums. A poor widow came and put in two small copper coins, which are worth a penny. Then he called his disciples and said to them. "Truly I tell you, this poor widow has put in more than all those who are contributing to the treasury. For all of them have contributed out of their abundance; but she out of her poverty has put in everything she had, all she had to live on.""*

It is ridiculous to think that such a bauble could be of any value, and yet Jesus is saying that it is, and it is said that sometimes the amount given was called out, in which case it would have caused a smile on some of the hearers' faces.

## *A Person Leaving the Temple – Matt 5,23-24*

*"So when you are offering your gift at the altar, if you remember that your brother or sister has something against you, leave your gift there before the altar and go; first be reconciled to your brother or sister, and then come and offer your gift."*

This would according to Jewish custom, be quite impossible and therefore containing some humour. It may be compared to someone coming up for Communion and just before receiving it running away to someone in the congregation who had something against them.

## *The Coat and the Cloak – Matt 5,40/Lk 8,29*

*"and if anyone wants to sue you and take your coat; give your cloak as well"*

*"If anyone, strikes you on the cheek, offer the other also; and from anyone who takes away your coat do not withhold even your shirt."*

The usual way of describing a fully dressed person was to say that he or she was wearing a coat, a cloak and shoes. This meant that in Jesus' example the man would have given both his coat and his cloak and would have been standing in the court stark naked before the judge – a comical situation.

## *Pearls to Swine – Matt 7,6*

*"Do not give what is holy to dogs; and, do not throw your pearls before swine, or they will trample them under foot and turn and maul you."*

One would say today that one would not give a fillet steak to a rat or a squirrel to eat.

## *Man's power is limited – Matt 5,36*

*"And do not swear by your head, for you cannot make one hair white or black."*

Man is unable to change creation. One of the Jewish Rabbi's used to say that if all the nations acted together they could not make the wing of a raven white, or one might transpose it and say that nothing could make the green leaves of an oak tree yellow.

## *Doing what you are told – Lk 17,7-10*

*"Who among you would say to your slave who has just come in from ploughing or tending sheep in the field, 'Come here at once and take your place at the table'? Would you not rather say to him, 'Prepare supper for me, put on your apron and serve while I eat and drink; later you may eat and drink'?. Do you thank the slave for doing what was commanded? So you also, when you have done all that you were ordered to do, say, 'We are worthless slaves; we have done only what we ought to have done!' "*

For the slave to eat before the master has had his meal is an absurd and comical example.

## *The thief – Matt 24,43/Lk 12,39*

*"But understand this: if the owner of the house had known in what part of the night the thief was coming, he would have stayed awake and would not have let his house be broken into."*

This describes the ridiculous behaviour of a man who does not expect a thief to come unless he knows beforehand or in today's world unless he is informed by phone or e-mail.

## *Jesus promises John the Baptist – Matt 11,7-8*

*As they went away, Jesus began to speak to the crowds about John: "What did you go out into the wilderness to look at? A reed shaken by the wind? What then did you go out to see? Someone dressed in soft robes? Look, those who wear soft robes are in royal palaces".*

A dandy in the desert is rather like a man in evening dress paddling about in a rubber dingy on a rough sea.

## *A Camel and a Gnat – Matt 23,25-26*

*"You blind guides! You strain out a gnat but swallow a camel! Woe to you, scribes and Pharisees, hypocrites! For you clean the outside of the cup and the plate, but inside they are full of greed and self-indulgence. You blind Pharisees! First clean the inside of the cup, so that the outside also may become clean."*

If someone on the Sabbath day had eaten a flea or a gnat they were considered to have committed a serious sin. And Jesus is saying that one might just as well have swallowed a camel, which is quite ridiculous of course, as having eaten a minute thing such as a gnat. It becomes a humorous paradox.

# *Chapter 5 – Conclusion*

I t has been said that our lives are helped by both genuine religion and genuine humour and in Chinese teaching the two forms are conjoined. It is my hope that these extracts endorse this view, and it is underlined in the concluding paragraph by Fr James Martin's book, "Between Heaven and Mirth":-

*"Preparation for heaven forms the basis of a great deal of Christian theology. Life, in this understanding is not so much a test as it is a rehearsal. And one way of preparing for something is by doing it. You get ready for a Little League tryout by practicing your pitching, batting and fielding. You rehearse for a concert by playing your instrument at home. You prepare for a wedding with a rehearsal the night before.*

*In this case, why couldn't earthly joy, humour, and laughter be a way of preparing for a lifetime of happiness? Why not allow yourself to enjoy a little heaven on earth? Engaging in those virtues, then, is not simply a way to live a fuller spiritual life now, but to orient yourself to your future.*

*So be joyful. Use your sense of humour. And laugh with the God who smiles when seeing you, rejoices over your very existence, and takes delight in you, all the days of your life."*

# THE CHOLESTEROL SOLUTION GUIDE:

## Lower Your Cholesterol in 30 Days Without Drugs

# Table Of Contents

# Introduction

I want to thank you and congratulate you for downloading the book, *The Cholesterol Solution Guide: Lower Your Cholesterol in 30 Days Without Drugs.*

This book contains proven steps and strategies on how to lower your cholesterol the natural way in just 30 days.

It will also tell you what cholesterol is, its signs, symptoms, causes, and types, so that you will be aware of the need to reduce your LDL or bad cholesterol levels and increase the HDL or good cholesterol levels. This information can very well save your life.

Thanks again for downloading this book; I hope you enjoy it!

# Chapter 1 What is Cholesterol?

Our liver, as well as other cells in our body, makes a fat-like and waxy substance called cholesterol. Aside from this natural production, there are also certain foods we take in that have cholesterol in them and these include meat, eggs, and dairy products.

For it to work properly, the body needs some cholesterol. Its cells' walls or membranes need cholesterol so as to create Vitamin D, hormones, and bile acids that will assist in digesting fat. The body however, necessitates only a certain amount of cholesterol. Too much cholesterol can create different health problems such as hypertension, heart attacks, and strokes.

Plaque, which is hard and thick, forms in your arteries when your body has excessive cholesterol. It restricts the area to your heart, making it difficult for blood to pass through. Later on, this buildup will lead to a condition called atherosclerosis, the hardening of your arteries. It will then result in heart disease.

Our blood carries the necessary oxygen to the heart but with too much cholesterol, this is difficult to do. It results in angina or pain in the chest. If the blood supply to your heart is totally cut off due to a blockage in the coronary artery, you will suffer from a heart attack.

Cholesterol is transported via your blood connected to a certain protein called lipoprotein. The latter is classified into three types:

1.  High density lipoprotein (HDL)

2.  Low density lipoprotein (LDL)

3.  Very low density lipoprotein (VLDL)

LDL is considered the bad cholesterol because it leads to plaque accumulation on the artery walls. If you have more LDL in your blood, you are more at risk of heart disease.

HDL is the good cholesterol because it assists the body in eliminating LDL in your blood. If you have a higher HDL cholesterol level, this is beneficial to you. If your HLD level is low, you are all the more prone to heart disease.

If you have VLDL, you are also susceptible to heart disease because this is similar to LDL. It has more fat and not much protein. VLDL carries triglycerides, a certain kind of fat, in your blood. Too much alcohol, sugar, and calories in your body are turned into triglycerides. They are then stored in your fat cells all over the body.

There are different factors which affect your cholesterol levels. One of them is diet. If you continuously have a diet that is filled with cholesterol and saturated fat, this can increase your cholesterol level. You should therefore minimize cholesterol and saturated fat in your meals.

Another factor which affects cholesterol level is weight. If you are overweight or obese, you have a higher risk of suffering from heart disease. This is because weight increases cholesterol levels. You should therefore lose weight so as to minimize LDL levels and boost HDL cholesterol.

It is advisable to exercise regularly because this increases HDL cholesterol and reduces LDL cholesterol. The target is to exercise half an hour five times a week.

When you age, cholesterol levels rise. The total cholesterol levels of premenopausal women are lower than that of males of a similar age. Once women reach menopause, their LDL levels tend to increase.

If you are suffering from diabetes and do not control it, your cholesterol levels will rise. If you control it though, your cholesterol will fall.

Heredity also plays a huge role in having high

cholesterol levels. There are families that have high blood cholesterol because it is in their genes. Other causes of high cholesterol levels are medical conditions and some medications.

If you are 20 years old or above, you should have your cholesterol level measured once every 5 years. Physicians say that a person's cholesterol level should remain below 200. If it goes beyond that, you will need to undergo lifestyle changes or take certain medications to lower your LDL cholesterol.

# Chapter 2 Symptoms and Effects of High Cholesterol

Knowing the symptoms of high cholesterol is vital because it will alert you if you are indeed suffering from this condition. When you are well-informed, you will know what treatment to use to help save your life.

Usually, high cholesterol symptoms are unnoticed by the sufferers. When plaque forms on your artery walls because of cholesterol buildup, the arteries begin to narrow. Physical symptoms will then show up later.

When your cholesterol levels go up, you may see fat deposits in your tendons and beneath your skin.

Another symptom of high cholesterol is high blood pressure. The reason for this is because your heart needs to work harder for it to pump blood through your clogged artery walls.

Another symptom of a high cholesterol level is a heart attack. Your coronary arteries will be blocked because of the plaque buildup along your artery walls so your heart will not get enough oxygen and a heart attack eventually happens.

You may also suffer from gall stones if you have high cholesterol levels. Your liver is the one that excretes toxins like bile out of your system. It also removes extra cholesterol from your blood stream. If your bile has a high cholesterol level, it forms gall stones.

There are also eye conditions that will indicate if you have high cholesterol. If you suffer from an eye abnormality called arcus senilis where a white rim appears around your cornea, this is an indication of high cholesterol. Cholesterol and fat deposits cause such a condition. A life-threatening eye disease is Hollenhorst plaque that involves your retina. With this condition, cholesterol deposits that are situated on different body parts are freed and attach themselves to the eyes' blood vessels as plaque.

In order to know what your cholesterol level is, you need to undergo a blood test which will show your HDL, DLD, and triglycerides levels. Twelve hours prior to the test, you are not allowed to eat anything. After taking the test, your doctor will interpret the results of the test before he gives recommendations. If you have a cholesterol level above 200mg per blood deciliter, you may need to undergo lifestyle changes. If the result is a lot higher than this, you will have to take certain medications.

# Chapter 3 What Causes High Cholesterol?

There are different causes of high cholesterol. There are those that people can control, while there are others that are beyond our control.

One of the causes of high cholesterol is the type of food you eat. You should stay away from foods with a lot of cholesterol, saturated fat, and trans-fat. Replace these with fruits and veggies. Check out food labels so that you will know the amount of cholesterol and fat in foods you consume. Have a diet that is high in fiber and low in fat. There are a lot of people who think eating foods that are labeled "cholesterol-free" will not raise their cholesterol levels. This is a false claim because your body turns fats into cholesterol.

One of the foods that is enriched with fat is butter. Try to stay away from foods seasoned or prepared with butter such as croissants. Avoid foods that are fried because the grease in them leads to high cholesterol. Grill or steam your food instead of frying it so as to decrease cholesterol levels.

Another food that is enriched with cholesterol-causing fat is regular mayonnaise. You can replace this with its fat-free or low-fat version.

You can also use mustard in your sandwiches instead of mayonnaise.

Avoid red meats because they have a lot of animal fat in them, which leads to high cholesterol. Go for white meats instead like turkey or chicken. You can also eat vegetarian meat such as tofu, so as to minimize cholesterol levels.

Another food to stay away from is whole cheese made from whole milk because of its high fat content. Consume cheeses that are fat-free or made from 2% milk. Drink low-fat or non-fat milk for your dairy needs. You can also replace milk with rice or soy milk.

Control your weight so that the chance of having heart disease shall be lessened. Maintain the body weight ideal for your age, height and body frame. If you do not do much physical activity, this shall lower your HDL levels and heighten your LDL cholesterol.

There are causes of high cholesterol which you cannot control and one of them, as mentioned previously, is age. Women who are 55 years and above will see an increase in LDL cholesterol levels, while men who are 45 years and above will experience their LDL cholesterol levels shooting up. Biologically, females possess lower cholesterol levels as compared to males.

Familial hypercholesterolemia is also one of the uncontrollable causes of high cholesterol levels. This is a genetic condition wherein inherited genes affect the way our bodies metabolize bad cholesterol.

There are also other causes of increased LDL cholesterol. They include the following:

1. Smoking
2. Certain prescription drugs
3. Diseases like diabetes and hypertension, among others
4. Stress
5. Excessive alcohol consumption. The ideal alcohol consumption is one to two glasses a day because more than that can heighten cholesterol levels.

# Chapter 4  Cholesterol-Lowering Foods

One of the natural ways to reduce cholesterol in your body is to consume certain cholesterol-lowering foods and avoid those that raise cholesterol levels.

One of the foods that naturally lowers cholesterol is apples. They have soluble fiber which aids in reducing cholesterol by helping it go out of your body. To obtain the full benefits of apples, consume them with their skin. You can also drink apple juice to help lower your bad cholesterol.

You should also eat grapes because they have a compound which aids in lowering bad cholesterol levels in your body. All kinds of grapes have this benefit but the darker their skin, the more compounds they have. For maximum benefits, it is advisable to eat the darker grapes.

Because of their soluble fiber content that aids in reducing LDL cholesterol, you should also eat prunes and pears. Soluble fiber has the tendency to minimize cholesterol absorption which effectively lowers LDL cholesterol in your intestines.

You should also consume walnuts because they aid in lowering cholesterol due to their polyunsaturated fatty acids. When you eat a handful of walnuts per day, this shall greatly decrease cholesterol levels in the body. Do not consume more than what is recommended though because nuts, like walnuts, have a lot of calories. Consuming too many will result in weight gain.

Other nuts that have polyunsaturated fatty acids which aid in the reduction of cholesterol are almonds, pine nuts, hazelnuts, pecans, peanuts and pistachios. When you are making salad, use nuts and not croutons because nuts have more benefits and will not make you gain weight.

Omega-3 fatty acids also help lower cholesterol levels in the body. You can find such fats in fish like albacore tuna, herring, mackerel, salmon, sardines, and trout. Consume fish at least two times per week so that you can receive its maximum benefits. Broiling or baking fish is delicious and beneficial for you.

Other foods which reduce cholesterol are brown rice, soy products, cinnamon, oats and garlic because they all have cholesterol-lowering properties. Instead of eating white rice, consume brown rice. You can also place a pinch of cinnamon on your oatmeal, breakfast cereals, tea or coffee.

Instead of seasoning your meals with salt, season them with garlic. Consume soy milk if you do not want to drink regular milk. You can also consume breads and cereals that come from oats.

Every day, try to consume 1 ½ grapefruits so as to reduce your LDL cholesterol. Those who consume grapefruit daily reduce their cholesterol level by 7% in just a couple of months. Grapefruit has pectin which lowers cholesterol levels.

Include beans in your meals as regularly as you can. These beans include soybeans, lima beans, kidney beans, navy beans as well as other legumes which aid in controlling cholesterol levels. If you eat 1 ½ cups of beans daily, your bad cholesterol levels can go down by 22%.

# Chapter 5 Home Remedies to Lower Cholesterol

Bad and good cholesterols can be balanced the natural way using proper nutrition and home remedies. This is ideal for those who do not want to use prescription medications due to their side effects.

Consume not less than 8 glasses of water per day so that your kidneys will be stimulated to remove toxins, especially the excess LDL cholesterol. There are also water mixtures you can drink to lower cholesterol. Squeeze the juice of an onion and add this to one glass of water. Do this once a day so as to regulate the rhythm of your heart and cleanse your blood.

Aside from onion juice, you can also add to a glass of water one teaspoon of fresh ground coriander. Drink this once each day to reduce your blood cholesterol level and motivate the kidneys to release toxins.

On your abdomen, place a mud pack once every day so as to improve kidney performance, liver function, and digestion. This will also stimulate the body to flush out toxins that are stored in your fat cells. It also minimizes overall stress as well as enhances heart function.

There are also supplements and teas that will help reduce your bad cholesterol levels. One of them is a fish oil capsule due to its omega-3 fatty acids. Take this before you go to bed every night so that your LDL cholesterol and triglyceride levels will be lowered. You can also consume one Indian bedillium capsule every day so as to maintain the LDL to HDL ratio of cholesterol in your body.

Boil 5 cups of water with 10 sticks of cinnamon and a teaspoon of honey. Drink this as tea once daily. You can also boil 2 cups of water mixed with a couple of teaspoons of coriander. Strain and then drink this as tea twice a day.

# Chapter 6 Lowering Cholesterol with Fiber

Fiber consumption is one of the ways to reduce cholesterol. It has two forms and they are soluble and insoluble fibers. Soluble fiber dissolves in water while insoluble fiber does not.

Cholesterol levels can be controlled by soluble fiber because it traps cholesterol, takes it away from one's body, and makes its production slower. The moment food gets into your intestines, your liver discharges bile coming from cholesterol so as to assist in digesting the food. Once soluble fiber is dissolved, it produces a substance which catches dietary cholesterol as well as bile and keeps them from going to the blood stream. The fiber is not absorbed by the body but instead, it goes out along with cholesterol when you defecate.

After bile and dietary cholesterol are removed, your body will utilize blood cholesterol for different purposes. This will then minimize your blood cholesterol levels. The dietary fiber stays in your intestines and ferments. As this happens, the bile's cholic acid is broken into chenodeoxycholic acid, a type of fatty acid. It inhibits the production of cholesterol in your liver, resulting in an overall reduction of your blood cholesterol levels.

The other kind of fiber, called insoluble fiber, will not attach to cholesterol. However, it will assist in eliminating waste. Soluble fiber will stop cholesterol absorption while insoluble fiber quickly takes it away from your body.

Medical experts say to add ten grams of soluble fiber every day to your diet so as to reduce LDL cholesterol. Others say women should add 25 grams of soluble fiber to their diet while men should add 38 grams.

You can find fiber in plants such as beans, fruits, and veggies. You can also find them in cereals, bread, and dairy products that are fiber-fortified. For easier intake of this nutrient, you should eat fresh fruits and veggies at every meal. Consume five to six small meals that have fiber-enriched foods. Take fiber slowly because it cannot be digested. When you take in too much fiber too quickly, it will result in bloating, discomfort, and gas.

# Chapter 7 Oatmeal for Cholesterol

The digestive tract soaks up bad cholesterol. Eating oatmeal has been proven to reduce LDL cholesterol from the body. It has soluble fiber that becomes sticky like paste as soon as it is added to liquid. This paste fastens to the intestine's bile acids and transports them out of the body as waste. It is cholesterol that makes up these bile acids. Since fiber delays digestion, the intestines fail to take in cholesterol in time to stop it from exiting.

Because oatmeal takes away cholesterol from your body, artherosclerosis is prevented. As we recall, this condition occurs when cholesterol builds up in your artery walls and turns into plaque. Oatmeal does not decrease the plaque existing in the arteries. Regular exercise and having a proper diet, of which oatmeal should be a part of, does.

According to the FDA, if you include foods having soluble fiber in your low-fat and low-cholesterol diet, this can lower the chance of suffering from heart disease. Back in 1977, a study showed that the soluble fiber found in oats reduced LDL cholesterol. The FDA then officially announced that oatmeal can lower bad cholesterol.

The easiest way to get insoluble fiber to your diet is by eating oatmeal of all kinds such as instant, cooked, muesli, porridge and other recipes that use rolled oats. You can also find soluble fiber in fruits and veggies such as apples, barley, beans, carrots, oranges, peas and psyllium. All these reduce your cholesterol levels but cooked oatmeal has the most amount of soluble fiber.

At an average, Americans consume only three to four grams of soluble fiber per day which is below the five to ten grams recommended amount. To have more soluble fiber for a healthy heart, eat an apple and some lima beans with your oatmeal.

In addition, if you wish to eat oatmeal for the purpose of reducing your cholesterol level, do not add sugar to it. For sweetening, you can use artificial sweetener or better yet, a sweet fruit such as strawberries or bananas.

You should consume half a cup of oatmeal per day so as to receive the health benefits of oatmeal. Consume this every breakfast and look for yummy recipes from the Internet to make a scrumptious oatmeal recipe with your favorite fruit.

You can also add flax seed in your diet if you are serious about lowering your cholesterol level. Once your oatmeal is cooked, add a couple of teaspoons of flax seed in grounded form. You can grind flax seed using a coffee grinder. Never cook flax seed because cooking it will remove its health benefits.

You can also combine soy milk, non-fat or low-fat milk to your oatmeal for added flavor. Oatmeal can be plain and bland but if you add some healthy ingredients to it, you will find that it is a delicious way of reducing cholesterol levels the natural way.

# Chapter 8 Barley and Cholesterol

It has been mentioned in this book that whole grains can help reduce cholesterol levels and should therefore be a part of one's diet. According to recent studies, barley is the most effective in reducing cholesterol levels among whole grains. Barley has soluble fiber the way oats do, particularly the soluble fiber called beta-glucan.

Be aware that when you consume food enriched with beta-glucan and other soluble fibers, it must only be eaten and never taken in pill or supplement form. If you consume too much barley however, you will experience gas and feel bloated even if this reduces your cholesterol level by 10%. This is according to a study done by clinical nutritionists.

Aside from making barley and other soluble fibers a part of your diet for cholesterol reduction, you should also decrease your intake of saturated fats. You can consume hot cereals from barley rather than oatmeal to gain its health benefits. You can boil four cups of water mixed with a teaspoon of cinnamon and half a cup of barley for 45 minutes. Mix in two cups of unsweetened apple juice and a tablespoon of lemon juice to this. Cook this for another half an hour or until the mixture has thickened and the liquid is fully absorbed.

During lunch and dinner, you can replace simple carbohydrates such as potatoes or white rice with cooked barley so as to help lower your cholesterol. You can make this as a side dish so that you will feel full. This will help you maintain a diet that is low in calories and at the same time, reduce your cholesterol.

Utilize barley flour rather than wheat flour when baking bread and other goods. This may have undergone processing but rest assured this still has beta-glucan in high levels. For snacks, you can consume barley flake cereal rather than processed foods such as chips.

According to health experts, barley water has been consumed since ancient times for medicinal purposes. Aside from lowering cholesterol levels, it protects the intestines and safeguards the body from diseases. There are glutinous particles that come from cooked barley which remain in your water once you strain out the grain. You can take this as an alternative to coffee or teas. You can add sugar, lemon, or orange rind to barley water for a healthy and delicious drink.

# Chapter 9 Red Yeast Rice For Cholesterol Reduction

Red yeast rice has been approved by health experts to treat high cholesterol. This is because of the presence of strong scientific evidence supporting its claim of reducing cholesterol levels. This kind of supplement comes from a certain kind of yeast growing on rice. It has monacolins that are said to have the ability to lower cholesterol. Red yeast rice can be found in health food shops. Many prescription medications for cholesterol actually have red yeast rice as an ingredient.

Before you buy a nutritional supplement that has red yeast rice, you should first get clearance from your doctor. The Food and Drug Administration does not control the selling of such dietary supplements so there are some products on the market that do not work well or may even interact with medications you are on. Your doctor will be able to tell you which supplement to buy and will advise you if taking this will be helpful or harmful to you.

If you are under 18 years old, you should not consume supplements with red yeast rice. The studies that were conducted on such supplements were done on people above 18 years old. If you are expecting, nursing, or suffering from a liver disease, do not take this supplement. If you are on prescription medications for cholesterol which has red yeast rice, there is no use in taking such a supplement.

If you are cleared to take red yeast rice supplement, the recommended dosage is 1,200mg to be taken two times a day. You should drink a whole glass of water with the pill. Make sure you take this with a meal. Never go beyond 2,400mg a day of this supplement unless your doctor advises you to do so. Take this supplement until your cholesterol level goes down or until your physician advises you to stop.

If you experience any side effects, tell your doctor. There are those who have suffered from abdominal pain, headaches, heartburn, bloating and gas with red yeast rice. It is also said to increase the risk of bleeding.

In order to effectively reduce cholesterol levels, you should have a proper diet and regular exercise regimen along with your red yeast rice supplementation. There are patients who lowered their cholesterol level minus prescription medications by consuming a lot of fiber, minimizing their intake of foods that have fat and cholesterol and exercising regularly.

There are some things you need to know if you are considering red yeast rice supplementation. Back in 2007, there were certain over-the-counter supplements enriched with red yeast rice that were banned by the FDA. These certain brands had lovastatin which was a usual ingredient in prescription medication for cholesterol. If you buy such a supplement, check if it has lovastatin because it is questionable as to whether this ingredient can really reduce cholesterol.

# Chapter 10 Eggplant and Cholesterol

One of the unique vegetables is an eggplant because of its beauty, color, taste and nutritional benefits. It is a vegetable that can reduce cholesterol in less than a month.

According to recent studies, those who consumed eggplant juice greatly reduced their bad LDL cholesterol levels. Their blood flow improved because their blood vessels' walls relaxed. This is because of the terpene and nasunin phytonutreints in them which help get rid of free radicals. In this chapter you will learn about a couple of the recipes you can make at home using eggplants so as to lower your bad cholesterol level.

When you shop for eggplants, get those that are firm, hard, and blemish-free. Once at home, wash them properly so as to take away residue or dirt. Take away the blossom ends and stem and then slice the vegetable diagonally into ½-inch pieces. Put the eggplant slices, along with lemon slices, in half a gallon of water. Refrigerate this for seven days and consume three glasses of this juice every day. Refill the container with water as needed. Do this for a month and you shall see your cholesterol levels lowering the natural way by not less than 20 points. You may find the water bitter so you can counteract the taste by taking a teaspoon of natural honey afterwards. For the next four weeks, you will need around four eggplants.

If drinking eggplant juice does not suit you, you can add this vegetable to your meals. You can have this fried, grilled, marinated, roasted or stuffed and mixed in stews, casseroles or on your brochettes. For additional flavoring in your eggplant dishes, you may add allspice, bay leaves, basil, chili powder, garlic, onions, oregano, parsley, sage, and tomatoes. Your cholesterol level can still be lowered but it will take a bit longer than a month.

If you are suffering from allergies or gallbladder and kidney problems, avoid eggplants. Before you go on with this natural remedy, always have clearance from your doctor first.

# Chapter 11 Cinnamon and Cholesterol

In a study conducted by a Maryland research center that involved 60 Type 2 diabetes sufferers who had cinnamon in their diets every day, scientists found astonishing results. The total cholesterol of the subjects was significantly reduced by the cinnamon in forty days. Their LDL cholesterol levels, triglycerides, and serum glucose all improved. Because of this, they deduced that cinnamon can lower cholesterol levels.

One recipe you can make with cinnamon is tea. In one cup of boiling water, infuse a teaspoon of ground cinnamon for not less than ten minutes. Take the liquid off and remove the solid at the bottom of your cup. You can sweeten the tea with a bit of apple juice. If you do not like tea, you can add one teaspoon of cinnamon in your ground coffee prior to brewing.

You can also add cinnamon to your meals. You can mix this in your chicken, beef, fish, and vegetable dishes. Look for cinnamon recipes on the Internet or in your cookbook. You will still receive the benefits of cinnamon although brewing it as tea is the quicker way to have your cholesterol levels go down.

You can also have cinnamon during dessert by adding it to your cakes, pies and cookies, among others. One teaspoon of cinnamon contains the equal amount of antioxidants in a cup of blueberries. Look for recipes for dessert that have cinnamon in them. Choose desserts that are fruit and vegetable-based as they are healthier.

You can also consume cinnamon in its capsule form which you can find in health food stores. This is an easier way of supplementing with cinnamon although it is more enjoyable eating delicious cinnamon dishes.

Cinnamon can also be utilized as a condiment. You can prepare fresh fruit and vegetable salad and add cinnamon to the vinaigrette. You can also sprinkle a dash of it on your hot chocolate drink or on your toast every morning. Top your spicy chili with a little bit of cinnamon. Have a bottle of cinnamon on your dining table so that you can always sprinkle it on your food and help lower your cholesterol levels.

Back in 2003, researchers from Pakistan also conducted a study of Type 2 diabetes patients who consumed a bit of cinnamon every day. It was found that their cholesterol levels also went down. Those who took one to six grams of cinnamon for forty days had their overall cholesterol levels reduced by 12% to 26%. Their LDL cholesterol levels and triglyceride levels improved. From this study, researchers said it is best for people with Type 2 diabetes to take cinnamon every day so as to minimize the chance of getting cardiovascular disease. The experts also said everyone should include cinnamon in their daily diet.

Succeeding studies were not able to prove the cinnamon-cholesterol treatment. Nutritionists from Harvard still say that the drug called statins is the best treatment for cholesterol reduction. Other researchers say that cinnamon has not yet been tested on the general populace. They also said that the cinnamon sold in supermarkets was not yet tested as well.

# Chapter 12 Garlic and Cholesterol

A lot of people have said that garlic can help lower high cholesterol levels. Although studies on this are inconclusive, many who have tired garlic as a cholesterol reduction home remedy have sworn to its effectiveness. You can try this remedy if you wish, but read the rest of this chapter first before you do.

Garlic is a close relative of onions and leeks. For many centuries now, it has been utilized as an herbal medication for different conditions. A very common claim is the tendency of garlic to reduce cholesterol levels. This herb is an antioxidant which prevents the oxidation of LDL cholesterol and keeps it from accumulating on the walls of the arteries.

A recent study in 2007 said raw garlic as well as garlic supplements had no significant effects when they were tried on cholesterol. There are other studies however that said one gram of garlic per day can reduce cholesterol by 20 milligrams per deciliter. There are also studies suggesting that this effect may just be temporary.

The ingredient in garlic which makes it reduce cholesterol levels is allicin. This is also found in leeks, onions, and shallots and it blocks sulfhydryl enzymes. These enzymes help manufacture the body's cholesterol.

You can use garlic in different recipes. You can sauté, fry and marinate with chopped, crushed, minced, pickled or roasted garlic. You can mix it in your salads, sauces, and soups. You can also add it to baked potatoes and pasta in its raw form.

An agricultural study said freshly crushed garlic is more potent than dried garlic. Garlic that is crushed will release the chemical messengers called hydrogen sulfide. These relax your blood vessels so more blood can pass through.

Before you use garlic to reduce your LDL cholesterol, ask your physician first. He would be able to give a full explanation of the benefits of garlic as compared to other chemicals or natural remedies. You may also be on medications like blood thinners which garlic can interact with in a negative way. It is therefore imperative that you tell your doctor about your desire to use garlic. According to some studies, consuming above .25 grams of garlic for every kilogram of your body weight can destroy your liver. It is therefore advisable to remain below this limit.

# Chapter 13 Apple Cider Vinegar and Cholesterol

One of the natural methods of reducing cholesterol is the consumption of apple cider vinegar. This is because of its ingredient called pectin, a soluble fiber. Pectin, which is not present in white vinegar, is from the apples that are used to make this vinegar. If you take apple cider vinegar orally, pectin will bind itself to cholesterol and fat and help flush them out of your body. It does not let these two build up and create havoc in your body.

Because pectin absorbs cholesterol and fat and eliminates them out of the body, your cholesterol level will be reduced and will not reach a harmful level. Since pectin is soluble in water, it adds bulk and shall make you feel full for a longer period. Your body will then be alerted that it is no longer hungry so you refrain from eating. If you eat less, you consume less cholesterol and this shall help manage its levels.

There are also amino acids in apple cider vinegar which reduce the effects of the bad cholesterol. They help your body remove them on its own.

A lot of individuals have had their cholesterol levels lowered by consuming one tablespoon of this vinegar daily. They also lost weight with it. Recommendations as to the amount of apple cider vinegar to be taken must be based on weight as well as the ability to bear its taste. To help lower cholesterol, you should take one tablespoon of it three times daily. You can also add a tiny amount of honey to it to make the vinegar taste better.

You can also add apple cider vinegar to your tea in the morning. Here's a tip that can help you handle its bitter taste: when you see that your cup is almost empty, add one tablespoon of apple cider vinegar and consume it all in one gulp.

For lunch, you can have salad with apple cider vinegar as dressing instead of your usual ranch. Not only will this eliminate a lot of fat from your diet but you are putting an ingredient in your body which will help flush fat and cholesterol from your system.

You can also add apple cider vinegar to your cooking. Instead of using white vinegar, go for apple cider vinegar. This will help reduce your cholesterol level by five points per month. In the process, you also lose a few pounds.

You can also add apple cider vinegar to your juice and drink it before going to bed. Mix a tablespoon of this to your grape or apple juice. This will make you have an additional dose of apple cider vinegar for the day and have your cholesterol lowered even more.

Before you supplement with apple cider vinegar, do get clearance from your doctor.

# Chapter 14 Red Wine and Cholesterol

Those who love to drink red wine will like what they read in this chapter. Red wine can actually reduce cholesterol levels, just as long as it is consumed moderately. One to two glasses of red wine a day will postpone your visit to your cardiologist.

When compared to other alcoholic drinks, red wine seems to be the healthier option. This is because it contains polyphenols which are antioxidants coming from grape skins. According to a study on red wine, this assists in reducing bad cholesterol levels and heightens good cholesterol levels in the body. It also revealed that those who regularly drank red wine had increased levels of HDL cholesterol. Research on red wine indicated that it has properties which can definitely reduce LDL cholesterol.

One other study isolated some chemicals that were said to be in red wine and can reduce bad cholesterol levels. These isolated chemicals are known as saponins found in grape skin and they are compounds that are glucose-based. Saponins are present in white and red wines but they are excessively higher in red wines. They are said to bind to cholesterol and prevent it from being absorbed by the body. The recommended dosage of saponin per day is 15mg, and you can find 7mg of it in just one glass of red wine.

Reservatrol is present in red wine. This is a chemical which prevents cholesterol oxidation in the body. The cholesterol levels shall then be decreased from the blood stream. This ingredient also stops the blood vessels from being damaged by the buildup of cholesterol.

Flavanoids are also found in red wine and this is said to prevent fats from being deposited on the arterial walls due to high cholesterol. There is still ongoing research about flavanoids so as to assess if it does have properties that lower cholesterol. It is however believed that they do help decrease some effects of having high cholesterol.

You should still be cautious about drinking red wine to prevent cholesterol buildup in the body. All doctors will tell you that alcohol should only be consumed in moderation. If you mix alcohol with drugs and other substances, this can lead to other health problems such as alcoholism. Women should drink just one 5-ounce glass of red wine each day, while men must limit red wine intake to two glasses per day.

# Chapter 15 Cranberry and Cholesterol

There are many people who use cranberry in order to lower their cholesterol level. The right amount of cholesterol is vital to the blood system because it helps repair tissues, produce steroid hormones and toughen cell membranes. If there is too much cholesterol in the body, this can be harmful to the health. Cranberry in your diet can help you maintain cholesterol levels at the right level.

Drink cranberry juice so as to decrease the possibility of acquiring cardiovascular disease. Cranberry has antioxidants which are good for the body. You can drink eight ounces of this juice every day but if you want effective results, drink three tall glasses of cranberry juice each day. When you have three glasses of cranberry juice daily, your good cholesterol will increase by 10%. According to studies, cranberry juice has 27% pure cranberry.

The bad cholesterol decreases with continued consumption of cranberries because of their phenols content. These are chemicals that effectively safeguard the arteries from the accumulation of plaque. Cranberry also has anthocyanins, flavonols and proanthocyanidins which stop LDL cholesterol oxidation. When you have an enormous supply of flavonoids, this shall minimize the ability of cholesterol to cling to your arteries.

To have a healthy breakfast, you can combine cranberries with oatmeal. Place 1 and ¼ cups water and half a cup rolled oats in your saucepan. Boil this mixture over medium-low heat and cook this for four minutes. Make sure to stir your oats so that they will not stick. Mix in ¼ cup non-fat milk and then cook for a couple of minutes. Always stir constantly.

Take your saucepan from the burner and add ¼ cup dried cranberries as well as fourteen chopped whole unsalted almonds. Top your oatmeal with one teaspoon of brown sugar. Here's a helpful tip, do not use instant oats because they are less effective in reducing cholesterol level.

Cranberries are more effective in reducing cholesterol levels than red grapes, according to studies. Therefore, use cranberries more often than red grapes.

Make sure that when you purchase cranberry juice concentrate, get the unsweetened kind. Add water to it and then sweeten with honey or non-aspartame sweetener. This is less costly than low-calorie juices containing chemical sweeteners.

Make sure to let your doctor check your cholesterol levels often and then heed his advice regarding diet, prescription medications, and natural remedies in reducing cholesterol levels.

# Chapter 16 Lemon Juice and Cholesterol

Many people use lemon juice when they cook their dishes; little do they know that lemon juice has many health benefits like maintaining liver health as well as reducing cholesterol levels. It is therefore beneficial if you add this juice to your everyday diet.

Lemon juice is healthy because of its special properties. Lemons have compounds known as limonoids that are usually found in citrus fruits. Limonoids make citrus fruits such as grapefruit and lemons bitter. A particular kind of limonoid called limonin has been found to lower cholesterol.

One study conducted in the latter part of 2007 said 80% of the body's cholesterol is produced in our liver, and the cholesterol is built with triglycerides and the substance apolipoprotein. Limonin slows down the manufacture of triglycerides and apolipoprotein. In addition, lemons are enriched with Vitamin C which is a very potent antioxidant that significantly lowers cholesterol levels in the body after a month of supplementing with it.

It is important to know how lemon juice should

be used so as to lower cholesterol levels in the body. Instead of the usual dressings loaded with fat that you mix with your salad, use lemon juice instead. You can also sauté your vegetables, fish or chicken in lemon rather than butter.

Drink lemon juice instead of sodas or other artificially-sweetened fruit juices. Get a fresh lemon, rinse it well and roll it on your countertop so you can get the most juice out of it. Cut it in half and then squeeze out the juice into a cup of hot or warm water. Drink this every day so that your cholesterol levels will go down. Your vitamin C intake will also increase with lemon juice.

Again, before you use lemon juice to bring down your cholesterol level, ask the approval of your doctor. You may be on medications that lemon juice will interfere with. You may also be suffering from other health problems which citrus fruits such as lemon will only worsen.

# Chapter 17 Juice Drinks for Lowering Cholesterol

Your battle against high cholesterol can actually be fought in a delicious and healthy way using the antioxidants in fruits and veggies. These antioxidants assist in lowering the effects of free radicals and stopping them from destroying our tissues. They also help in preventing arteries from being blocked and cholesterol levels from going up. When you juice fruits and vegetables, you can get huge amounts of these antioxidants in your diet.

For breakfast, you can have an apple-celery juice. Get two unpeeled apples, a cucumber and one stalk of celery and place them all in your juicer. Consume this every morning. The celery and apple juice can help fight cancer and lower cholesterol levels. It also helps in improving upset tummies and headaches.

You can also juice an apple and ginger. Combine one apple, four carrots, some parsley and a ¼-inch piece of ginger in your juicer. Later on, you can add one clove of garlic. The apple and carrots reduce cholesterol and counteract free radicals. Garlic and parsley are both enriched with antioxidants.

Have a spinach drink to lower your cholesterol. Juice some spinach, two celery stalks and two carrots. You can add a quarter of an apple or a small amount of orange juice for a sweeter taste. Spinach is enriched with antioxidants that control cholesterol levels.

A refreshing drink is watermelon juice. Juice together a couple of slices of watermelon, a tiny bunch of kale, and a broccoli floret of medium size. All of these are filled with antioxidants that fight off free radicals.

You can drink these juices any time of the day, as frequently as you want. The more you have them in your diet, the healthier you become.

# Chapter 18 Goat's Milk and Cholesterol

Goat's milk is the same as cow's milk except that the former is a healthier choice. It lowers cholesterol levels and has two times as many MCT or medium chain triglycerides which reduce cholesterol in the body.

Instead of drinking cow's milk, go for goat's milk. The latter has a stronger taste so you may want to mix them both at first. Later on, increase the amount of goat's milk till you are used to the taste.

Always go for the low-fat milk as opposed to its full-fat version. Although the fats in goat's milk are healthier, they are as high as those of cow's milk. To minimize total fat consumption, choose the low-fat version instead.

Consume yogurts and cheeses that come from goat's milk. Today, these are more preferred by people and they are now easier to purchase. These have a more appealing taste and have a smoother texture.

# Chapter 19 Herbal Remedies for Cholesterol

Because they are natural, herbs are considered to be very safe when it comes to treating health problems. Cholesterol can be lowered using herbal remedies. There are doctors who recommend specific herbs for reducing cholesterol levels and they are goldenseal, hawthorn, and turmeric. These should be consumed along with nutrients such as coenzyme Q10 and calcium. You should also maintain a healthy lifestyle that includes proper diet and regular exercise along with the consumption of these herbs.

An anti-inflammatory herb with cleansing properties, goldenseal can fight respiratory ailments. It also has the phytochemicals like beta-carotene as well as nutrients such as B-vitamins, magnesium, and zinc which all lower blood pressure and act the ways statins do. A study conducted in 2006 says goldenseal may be a valuable herb that effectively lowers cholesterol.

Hawthorn has seventeen phytochemicals including acetylcholine, pectin, catechin and beta-carotene. It also possesses a lot of valuable nutrients like amino acids, potassium, magnesium, and calcium. It opens up coronary blood vessels, strengthens the muscles of the heart and reduces cholesterol levels. It can lessen fatty deposits and is good for circulatory, high cholesterol, and cardiovascular disorders.

Turmeric is frequently used to reduce bad cholesterol levels and promote healthy circulation. It has phytochemicals such as beta-carotene as well as nutrients like calcium. There are some clinical trials on turmeric to show that it can combat high cholesterol levels.

Before trying any herb to reduce your cholesterol levels, always ask the advice of your doctor. You may be taking some medications that will interact with the herbs.

# Chapter 20 Vitamins and Cholesterol

Many natural remedies for cholesterol reduction have been mentioned in this book. In these chapters, the use of specific vitamins was stated. This chapter shall enumerate the different vitamins to take which are known to reduce cholesterol levels.

Have a Vitamin-B complex supplement which includes niacin, folic acid, and Vitamins B12 and B6. All these four are said to be "heart-healthy" and reduce cholesterol. Niacin has a unique quality of reducing the bad cholesterol as it increases the good cholesterol.

Have more vitamin C. This vitamin is a potent antioxidant and helps neutralize the free radicals entering our body before they connect with the bad cholesterol. This then minimizes the chance of acquiring heart disease and high blood cholesterol.

Your diet should have the plant-derived substances beta-sitosterol and sitostanol which help reduce cholesterol. These additives can be found in products like fruit juices and margarines.

Omega-3 fatty acids help reduce cholesterol

levels. As mentioned, this can be acquired from cold-water fish. There are also supplements that are filled with this healthy fat to help you have a healthy heart. When you take this every day in its correct dosage, you will see your cholesterol levels dropping.

Have more calcium in your diet because this lowers your cholesterol level by 2% to 4%. Further studies have yet to prove this claim though.

Ask your doctor for other vitamins that will help you lower your cholesterol levels. The ones mentioned in this chapter are the popular nutrients known to reduce cholesterol.

# Chapter 21 Exercise and Cholesterol

All medical experts will agree that a healthy diet along with regular exercise is one of the proven and most effective ways of reducing cholesterol levels. When you perform cardiovascular workouts like biking, dancing, running and swimming, these strengthen your heart muscles, lower your weight and heighten lung power. All these will help you when you have high bad cholesterol levels because your heart and lungs have to be strong to avoid coronary heart disease.

There are a lot of people who exercise half an hour three times a week and experience their LDL cholesterol going down while their HDL cholesterol goes up. In addition, frequent exercise helps maintain a good weight which is vital in fighting high cholesterol. When excess weight goes down, the bad cholesterol level also decreases.

Walking is one easy and inexpensive way for cholesterol to go down. You should walk at a 1.5mph to 2.5mph rate for half an hour, five to seven times a week. This is easy for a lot of people to do and does not have a huge impact on their joints.

Brisk walking will all the more reduce your cholesterol levels. You can walk up and down your stairs for half an hour or go around your neighborhood in the morning for an hour. The pace should be brisk enough for your heart rate to significantly increase. It is not enough to merely increase the amount of steps you take.

Another way to enjoy working out is to find a sport you enjoy and engage in it. Sport activities that involve a lot of physical movements are baseball, badminton, tennis, and frisbee. The secret is to have fun while playing because this will kill time and make you burn calories and fats.

# Conclusion

Thank you again for downloading this book!

I hope this book empowers you to lower your bad cholesterol level and raise the good cholesterol level.

Finally, if you enjoyed this book, please take the time to share your thoughts and post a review on Amazon. It'd be greatly appreciated!

Thank you and good luck!

Printed in Great Britain
by Amazon